Grace in One…

PASTOR YOUMONE AND MINISTER DAMIAN
BERRIEN

DEDICATION

To our Sanai Joi Bahndeh

"Weeping may endure for a night, but [Joi] comes in the morning."
Psalms 30:56

CONTENTS

Prologue i

1 GRACE TO *PUSH* 8

2 GRACE TO *GO* 16

3 GRACE TO *DECIDE* 26

4 GRACE TO *RELEASE* 32

5 GRACE TO *LOVE AGAIN* 41

6 GRACE TO *STOP* 45

7 GRACE TO *SPEAK* 50

PROLOGUE

Grace and Sufficiency

One of the greatest lessons we learned in the throes of coping with the loss of our daughter, Sanai Joi, was the blessing of asking for God's grace in segmented chunks. When asked, "How are you making it through this tough time?", our response was always, *"We pray for God's grace to get to the next second; and then after making it to the next second, grace to make it to the next minute; and then grace for the hour, and finally, grace to make it to the end of the day.* We no longer sought to answer the questions that rested in the realm of tomorrow, but only focused on the challenges that were presented to us in that moment.

Matthew 6:34 instructs us, "Therefore, do not worry about tomorrow, for tomorrow will worry about its own things. Sufficient for the day is its own". Tomorrow is what scared us. We had no answers for tomorrow; we barely could make it through the current day. It was in our fear of tomorrow that the Lord spoke to us about asking Him for His promised portion of grace. Grace, the free and unmerited favor of God, is what saved us from falling into the grave reserved for our daughter's remains.

We were reminded of the word of the Lord spoken to the Apostle Paul, "My grace is sufficient for you, for My strength is made perfect in weakness…" (2 Corinthians 12:9 NKJV). God's grace is sufficient, it is enough; His strength is working as it purposes to work when we are too weak to assist. When we began looking to fill our emptiness with the presence of family and friends (some of whom were insensitive to our grief), we were reminded that God's grace is sufficient. When we attempted to answer the daily questions unique to our survival, we were reminded that God's grace is sufficient. Even when we wondered how we would make it to and beyond her wake and funeral, God's Spirit whispered, "My grace is sufficient". It was this whisper that guided us in one of the most difficult journeys of our lives and will also carry you through the *next second, minute, hour, and day* of your journey.

1 GRACE TO *PUSH*

"For thou hast possessed my reins: thou hast covered me in my mother's womb. I will praise thee; for I am fearfully and wonderfully made: marvelous are thy works, and that my soul knoweth right well. My substance was not hid from thee, when I was made in secret, and curiously wrought in the lowest parts of the earth. Thine eyes did see my substance, yet being imperfect; and in thy book all my members were written, which in continuance were fashioned, when as yet there was none of them."

Psalm 139:13-16

 We prayed and waited for a baby girl after having two boys within 13 months of each other. Two years had gone by and we were prepared to again welcome another child, but even more ecstatic because this child was the long-awaited girl.

It was Valentine's Day 2011, 36 weeks gestation—the clearance date for a full term "normal" fetus. I felt sharp, repetitive pains prick within my abdomen. I nudged Damian, excitedly wanting to inform him of the contractions that were now five minutes apart.

Like the cases I've seen on television, he grunted a little and turned over in his sleep. I decided to get the bags and belongings together, as well as call my doctor in hopes that when he did awake, we wouldn't have any further delay. While on the phone with the doctor, I felt warm fluid flowing from below and realized my "water had broken". Now, I knew it was, "ready, set, go 'time'! And so did Damian. The nudge this time around was the insistent breaking news of, "my water broke!", prompting his swift reaction. He ran and got our boys dressed, grabbed the bags and met me in the car. Finally, our baby girl was on her way!

We arrived at the hospital in record time, with no delay of traffic (as expected, there was no one on the road at four o'clock in the morning, except us and truckers on their way to make long distance drop-offs to unknown places). Once checked in, I was separated from the men in my life, just the girls in the room…me, my doctor, and baby girl. Finally, Damian and the boys were permitted to enter and we all listened to the rhythmic kicking and moving sounds of Sanai's uterine orchestra. She was very active…strong heart and forceful kicks. The nurse told us her delivery would probably come more quickly than my previous labor and deliveries which totaled 44 hours of excruciating…"Joy". It was while waiting for the anesthesiologist to come, that we were reminded by the television newscaster that it was Valentine's Day, the day of love…and the perfect day to birth a representation of our love.

We were blessed to have my parents come and offer to take the boys home, get them dressed, and take them to daycare for us. We all knew that this would be an eventful day and we hoped it could be as calm as possible.

We never imagined the epidural would work so quickly. Before we knew it, they were moving in the infant bed and delivery equipment. Just as we prepared to call my parents and invite them to come back quickly, so as not to miss the rapid delivery of our Sanai Joi, the nurses barged in the room and began checking the fetal monitor and urging me to turn on my side because her heartbeat was no longer registering. After minutes of turning, checking, turning and re-checking, they paged the doctor and told me of the possible need for a Caesarean Section. I had never undergone such a procedure before and was filled with fear and unbelief. I peeked over at Damian for comfort and was met with a bloodless face consumed with the same fear and unbelief.

We prayed.

My doctor arrived and instructed the nurses to insert a flush into my uterus, perhaps the baby's umbilical cord was compressed and due to the fact that my water had broken earlier that morning, the lack of fluid was contributing to the cord's lack of mobility. *It made perfect sense to us at the time.*

The flush was unsuccessful and the doctor informed us of the dire need to "get the baby out" due to her decreasing heart rate. Just as she gave us a snapshot review of the C-section process, I dilated to 10 centimeters and she encouraged me to push. After three or four pushes, Sanai was out, and not breathing. For the first time in our labor and deliveries, Damian vomited on the floor. He was my rock through the birth of our two sons. He held my hand and encouraged me to push both boys out through the pain; he breathed and counted with me—as those faithful men do on television; he kissed my forehead and rubbed sweat from my brow; and thanked the Lord with me for the beautiful gifts He had given us. This time, he threw up and rushed to the in-room restroom. My foundation was shaken; my rock was broken.

***

I didn't know what to do; I was supposed to be her rock; I was supposed to be strong; I should have known what to do...what to fix. But, I couldn't. I threw up on the floor. The birth of my daughter made me throw up on the floor.

It wasn't supposed to be this way. We went to all the doctor's appointments and they said everything was okay. We watched as they performed three ultrasounds and after all of them, we left there thinking everything was good—our baby girl was healthy. Now, after waiting all of this time to meet the girl we had always prayed for, she comes out not breathing

and purple. This wasn't my baby girl! This wasn't the daughter I asked God for; the one that I would spoil and give all the finer things to; the one I would protect from all the boys in the neighborhood; the one I would walk down the aisle and the one that would bury me some day…this wasn't her!

I rejoined my wife at her side and we watched as the nurses tried to breathe life into our daughter's body. She was so small and pale under those lights. I didn't have a chance to hold her hand, kiss her cheeks or even see who she looked like. We had a running bet that she would look like me, since my genes were stronger…I guess no one won the bet that day. Once they got her breathing, they rushed her off to the NICU. My wife already knew I was following close behind them—I was still my daughter's protector…death wouldn't steal her away.

***

There were no tiny hands flailing because of the shock of leaving a warm womb for a frigidly cold hospital room; no wrinkled frown or gaze of anger from being evicted from a comfortable place for nine months; and there was no piercing cry of displeasure for being ripped from the place of peace, as experienced in my first two deliveries--there was silence; and that silence was, indeed, deafening. I could barely grab a glimpse of her as the doctor flipped her softly, then violently slapping her on her sagging purple bottom saying, "Come on, baby girl! You awake?

Come on baby girl, let us hear you!" We were frozen in that moment.

We watched as the Neonatal Intensive Care Unit Emergency Team rushed in with respiratory equipment, ready to resuscitate our semi-lifeless baby. My doctor allowed me to give her a quick kiss before relinquishing care to the NICU. Time slowed down long enough for me to take a snapshot of the fog of her face and drooped eyes. She was cold and leathery; my kiss left an imprint on her forehead. Minutes went by as her limp body lay on the small bed. Damian and I watched as the doctors attempted to force breath from her body. I paid no attention to the fact that I was still fully immersed in the delivery process with the doctor and the nurse tugging and massaging my stomach delivering the placenta. We finally heard a faint yelp and then she was placed in a transporter and rushed to the NICU. We were left in shock. I was left with remnants of a baby bump, no significant pain...and no baby.

The words of the doctor and nurses were comfortless and met with deep sobs of a heartbroken mom and dad. We didn't have a chance to call my mom and dad and warn them before they came back to the hospital with our boys, waiting to see the newest member of our family. They had so many questions that we were unable to answer, "What happened?", "Why wasn't she breathing?", "What did the doctor say?", "Can we see her?"...we were just as baffled as they were. Instead of calling family, friends and church members to reveal the sex, size, and selfies of our baby, we sent text messages asking them all to do the only thing we knew to do at the time, pray.

We all prayed; prayed for answers, prayed for healing, prayed for her life.

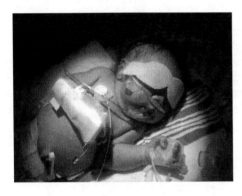 I waddled back and forth to the NICU those two days, even against the directions of the nurses pleading for my rest. I pumped "cc's" of colostrum every two hours (anxiously awaiting the "liquid gold" that would heal my baby). I held her tiny hand as she laid, dependent on the tube of air attached to her nose. She was beautiful. She looked just like my mom…and we had a beautiful dress waiting on her when she got home.

We began taking pictures of our "broken", but beautiful baby girl. We sat in the NICU and prayed; we prayed and we stared at her…stared and we prayed. Even the Specialists were puzzled by her condition. No one had the answers…except the Master.

We realized, God made her this way, and this was the walk for her life and subsequently our lives as well.

2 GRACE TO *GO*

"I will instruct you and teach you in the way you should go; I will counsel you with my eye upon you." Psalm 32:8

****

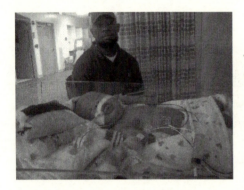

Sanai ended up looking just like me! I sat there staring at her with all those tubes in her nose, her stomach….all over her body. But, she was beautiful. She knew who I was when she looked in my eyes and when the lights were too bright, she knew my voice and breathed more calmly when I sang into her ear.

I couldn't think about working— I told my boss I needed time off. This was too much. My wife was still healing from the delivery, but wanted to go to the NICU every day, multiple times a day, just to see our baby girl. I couldn't focus on calling and harassing people about paying their car notes while my daughter struggled to grab each breath. I told my boss that I needed to stay on medical leave—I mean FMLA is for men, too, right? I also wondered, *How would my wife feel? Would she*

16

look at me like I was less of a man because I wasn't working? But, then again, how will I pay the bills…take care of the boys? I had plenty of questions, but very few answers. All I knew was that I had to be there for my daughter. I was her daddy. She needed me. I wasn't worried about that dead-end job.

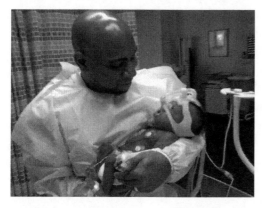

There was so much pressure in our lives. We were always busy, going back and forth from the hospital to dropping off our boys at school and flag football games, going to church, home, recreational activities with our boys and then back to the NICU again. I wanted things to be normal for our boys, but our world now revolved around Sanai and we needed to balance life as we now knew it around her. My wife won Teacher of the Year for her school district, which required us to attend meet-and-greet events, and other special engagements. I decided I would take her where she needed to go. If she needed a driver, I would be her chauffeur. She acted strong, but I knew deep inside she was weak and needed my shoulder and encouragement…so the least I could do was be present for her in those moments. I watched as her passion for teaching shined brightly in front of packed audiences, proud of her ability to smile even though I knew she was

hurting…because even I was hurting.

After waiting three weeks, the doctors told us she had Partial Trisomy Q, a genetic disorder. I couldn't figure out how they didn't know or see this problem with all of the ultrasounds they performed. They told us she was perfect; and now they changed her perfection to a death sentence, telling us babies like her don't live beyond their first year of life. *What? She won't live to see her first birthday? She's going to die? No!* I refused to accept this prognosis. I didn't care about the odds stacked against her, my daughter was going to make it…she had to.

****

We endured days of uncertainty, anxiety, worry, and frustration before being given the cause of her multiple ailments and deficiencies. At three weeks old, Sanai was diagnosed with Partial Trisomy Q, a chromosomal disorder that granted her months to live and promised her demise before her first birthday. She was diagnosed with a hole in her heart (of which she underwent surgery her first weeks of life), and enlarged tongue, which restricted her breathing and led to a tracheotomy, extra digits (12 fingers), and intestinal abnormalities as well (which led to the installation of a g-tube). She became dependent on a ventilator, even with moments of hope with weening her from the machine. Her frequent "episodes", as the nurses called it, would put her back on the machine and at a higher respiratory rate than before.

We still maintained hope. We successfully passed the training offered by the NICU team for tracheotomy and G-tube care, interviewed and selected a home health care company to assist with 24-hour care upon her discharge—I even pondered being a stay-at-home mom...whatever it took to keep my baby girl here, with me, alive and well.

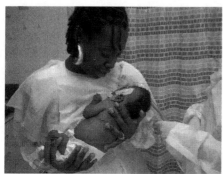

We visited the NICU every day (possibly missing a day every now and then due to exhaustion). We spent hours upon hours at her bedside and in the waiting rooms of operating rooms, praying for her recovery. We met and crossed each hurdle successfully together. We thanked God for her strength and the knowledge and skill of the medical team.

We did this for nearly four months. During those months, not only were we dealing with the 'highs and lows' of being NICU parents, but we were (by the grace of God) managing a busy life as parents of two other young children, employees, church ministry and community leaders. Our son had flag football games, so we all went as a family to games...and then to the NICU. We had church and bible study to attend, so we went as a family to worship services…and then to the NICU.

I won the title as the school district's Teacher of the Year, an unexpected surprise. It was soon after I gave birth that I was informed that I was one of the finalist for Teacher of the Year. The committee was insistent that I return to my classroom to teach a lesson so the judges could make their final determination—one of the requirements for consideration was that each finalist be observed one final time teaching in their classroom and scored according to their rubric. It seemed impossible to not only leave Sanai in her condition, as well as ignore the reality that I had not yet healed physically or mentally from giving birth, but to now go and teach a class. My mother spoke sternly to me and told me I had to fight to get what the enemy was trying to steal from me…she was right. It would have been easy to just sulk in my pain, feel sorry for myself, and luxuriate in my pity party, but God was calling me beyond misery and pain, and into purpose.

My family made sure I got to my school. My best friend worked out the details with the administration and made sure my students were prepared for my unexpected and brief return. Damian drove me there and had already warned me that I could only teach one class and he would be waiting in the main office to take me back home to rest. I appreciated his concern and sternness. I taught the class—my students were excellent—and the judges observed my instruction. They would come to a consensus and select the teacher that embodied the resilience, skill, passion and compassion representative of all teachers in the district. I left the school that day grateful that I made it to the top five finalist and was satisfied with being just that.

Throughout the next weeks, in between going back and forth to the hospital, the finalist met with the committee and received pertinent information regarding the upcoming ceremony. I, of course, missed all of the information and was surprised when I was told days before the big ceremony that the district chartered a school bus for myself and my special guests. I was under the impression that only adults could attend the event, so we arranged to have my god-sister babysit the boys for us—which meant Damian had to drop them off and meet me at the event. I rode a 55-passenger bus by myself to the Teacher of the Year awards ceremony. The driver and I conversed awkwardly during the course of my solo ride to the Performing Arts complex. As we pulled up to the red carpet drop off, the driver (probably feeling sorry for me) told me that she was rooting for me to win. She commented, "See, you the underdog. You don't have all these people and buses like the other people have. God is going to make sure you win!", as she pulled up behind the other charter buses packed with the finalists and their entourage of supporters. It all sounded good, but didn't feel that way. I was more concerned about getting through the night so I could visit Sanai— continuing our usual routine.

I met up with Damian, my parents, my best friend, and my Principal—those were the only supporters that joined me that day. I was, indeed, the underdog. My mom, in mom fashion, asked everyone around her to cheer me on when they called my name—I guess, she wanted me to feel the love I so desperately needed. After they showed my video showcase and after my students spoke about the impact I had made on their lives, I heard the room fill with applause…and love. I felt the love; and all of a sudden, the pain subsided temporarily and Damian and I were no longer alone fighting, we had others fighting with us.

I was completely taken aback when they called my name. I thought for sure one of the other finalist would have won—they were all so deserving, excellent educators, and just all around great people. But, God allowed me to win. I realized the gift in what Jesus told the young rich ruler, "and everyone who has left houses or brothers or sisters or father or mother or children or lands, for my name's sake, will receive hundredfold and will inherit eternal life. But many who are first will be last, and the last first" (Matthew 19:29-30, ESV). He had moved me from last to first, in my low state of pity, God had elevated me…all for His glory.

We tried to keep our sons' lives as normal as possible.

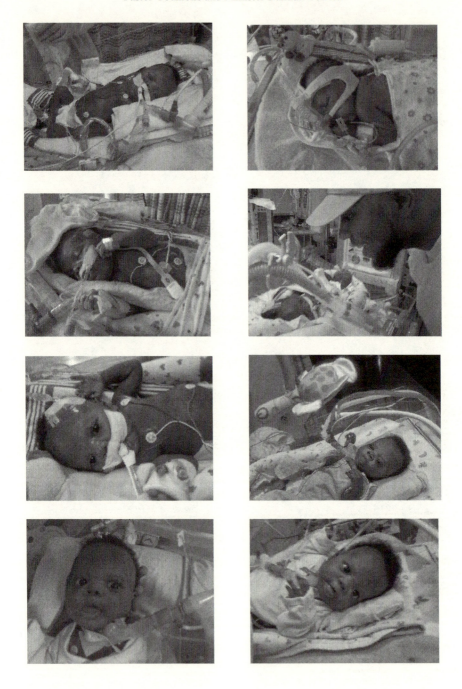

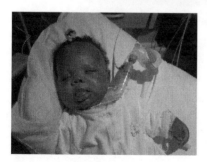 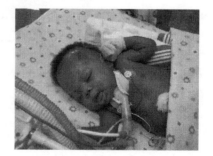

3 GRACE TO DECIDE

"Do not be anxious about anything, but in everything by prayer and supplication with thanksgiving let your requests be made known to God. And the peace of God, which surpasses all understanding, will guard your hearts and your minds in Christ Jesus." – Philippians 4:6-7

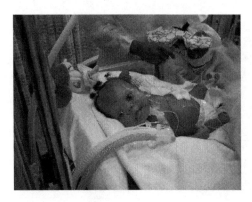 We were caught off guard on June 10 when the cardiologist, along with the geneticist told us that there was nothing else they could do for our baby and that we should begin planning for her demise. Tough news to take in for a young couple who had rededicated their lives and their marriage to the Lord, and had believed that God would heal their daughter and it would be but a matter of time before she joined them at home and made their family complete. We cried and questioned the doctor's findings, trying to make sense of an incomprehensible concept: our daughter was going to die.

We agreed on the 'Do Not Resuscitate' recommendation. I must admit, I was the first to tell the doctors, "No! Do everything you can for her!", so that she might live; knowing the final say wouldn't be had by me or the doctors.

I was shocked when Damian, who is normally reserved in opinion and critical decision making, raised his voice over my assertions and those of the doctors and said, "No! If you see that she is going, let her go." Throughout our five years of marriage he had no real opinion about where we would live, what schools the boys would attend, how much money was spent, what essentials needed to be bought…no voiced opinion.

I was accustomed to making the decisions; weighing the pros and cons; determining the options that would have lasting affects; resolving difficult situations from an objective, global perspective. He just sat by and obliged, shrugging his shoulder when asked of his opinion. Imagine my surprise when he gave birth to Assertion.

His rationale was simple, he didn't want her to feel the pain of a 100-plus pound adult pounding on her tiny heart, attempting to 'restart' her. So, I verbally agreed with him, inwardly resenting the decision he made for my daughter's life. I wanted to be the submissive wife we had heard about in church, (and even agreed to be her when asked by a marital counselor), but not in this decision…this was a real decision! However, God's divine muzzle covered my will and forced His will to be done.

***

The inside cry of a grown man, is louder than the outside yell of a heartbroken mother. I had to decide to let her go. They told us she wasn't going to make it. I mean, one day we're preparing for her next heart surgery and then the next day they tell us "there is nothing else we can do for her". A part of me wanted to punch this specialty doctor—a man we waited weeks to see and who only gave us bad news—and the other part of me wanted all of this to end. Sanai was tough; Sanai was strong; Sanai had gone through pain I, as a grown man, had never gone through; and I had to realize Sanai was tired.

Her mom, of course, didn't get it. She wanted to hold on to her and fight for her right to live…but what about her right to die? She didn't consider that. How selfish would it be for us to try and keep her here with us, suffering through life in constant pain, just so that we could see her each day? How cruel would it be for us to allow 200-pound adults to beat on her small baby to resuscitate her if she had decided to go home and be with the Lord? They told me about the potential of cracked ribs if they had to perform CPR, and I didn't want anything else broken on her…I wanted her to be whole, again.

So, I made the decision to sign the "Do Not Resuscitate" consent form—whether her mom liked it or not. She needed to

go home to be with the Lord and we had to let her go. One of us had to make a choice, and as her father, I knew it needed to be me. Her mother would have never let her go.

***

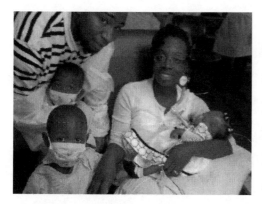

We all enjoyed the time spent with her that night during a NICU photoshoot arranged by the Chaplain and "Forget Me Not" Photography, a company that is known for capturing intimate moments that would last long beyond the sting of death. That night we brought her beautiful dress and engaged Sanai in her first and final photo shoot.

Our boys played with their sister for the first time. Throughout her time in the NICU, they stayed in the waiting room playing with building blocks and little wrestling and Army action figures made to play football and basketball on the plush carpet. Children were not allowed in the secure NICU ward. Damian and I would take turns waiting with them; we kept them there because her big brothers needed to be there, even if they couldn't see her. But, today was different. They were permitted to go back with us to her bedside and visit with their sister—to see if the pictures we would show them after visits did justice to her true beauty. They touched her face and rubbed her hair, amazed at how different she, a girl, was from them, yet so similar. They had questions about why she kept her tongue out of her mouth and why she couldn't talk back to them—they were young and I'm not sure our explanations were good enough.

My dad enjoyed his time with her as well. He had made sure he visited her nearly every day on his lunch breaks or if he was in the vicinity of the hospital. The nurses knew him. They would say, "your dad stopped by here today". Sanai knew her Grandpa's heavy, African accent when he bent over her bed to kiss her forehead. He wanted her to know that she belonged to him too—that she was his baby girl as well. He gave her the name "Bahndeh", because she was "the one for which we prayed".

Damian and I were able to hold our baby girl close to our heart without the canary yellow hospital gown separating us. Her stats appeared on the monitor as those of a healthy baby. Her breathing was perfect and her smiles illuminated the room. She had never had so many visitors there (at the same time) hanging onto every movement and gurgle. The staff had broken all the Visitor's rules, for our broken little girl, and had contributed to the ecstasy we experienced that night, as a family.

Grace in One

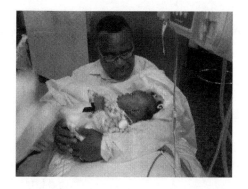

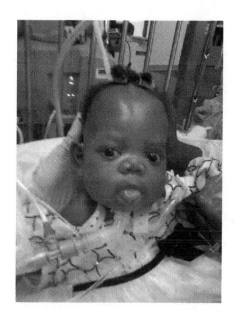

4 GRACE TO *RELEASE*

"I asked the Lord to give me this [daughter], and he has granted my request. Now I am giving [her] to the Lord, and [she] will belong to the Lord [her] whole life' and [we]worshipped the Lord there." 1 Samuel 1:27-28 NLT

June 11, 2011 came and brought eternity with it.

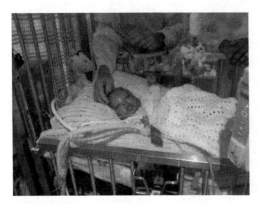

The walk into the NICU that morning was different; death lurked and hovered over her crib. Her heart rate and breathing was at an all-time low, her stomach and face were swollen (as her food would no longer pass through her g-tube), and her eyes were gazed. We had all gathered in the NICU that morning for the purpose of dedicating her to the Lord; but I then realized she had already embarked on her journey back to Him…without even asking my permission, and I must admit, I was mad at her. She had decided to be obedient to her Heavenly Father, instead of her mother.

My dad was absent at the Christening. We had exchanged heated words that morning because of a phone call I received from a distant church member sending her condolences on the DEATH of my daughter. She had received word that my daughter had already died, and was rather confused at my anger towards her. There was a small part of me that felt sorry for the wrath of Mother Youmone that rained on this poor, unsuspecting woman, but there was a greater zeal in me to set the record straight with everyone that "My daughter is not dead! She is alive!" ...at least for now. My father's apologies went without forgiveness as my belief in his own attempts to receive notoriety from my daughter's death strangled my need for him to join us in a display of the newness of life she would receive through her Christening.

I remember my mother standing up to her husband, my father, making the decision to be a support for her daughter in this difficult time, understanding the deadly mixture of emotions that can consume someone in a similar position. She and my aunt tried to convince him to set aside his feelings of rejection and come to the hospital to stand by his baby girl. But pride constrained him. Hindsight does, indeed, provide a clearer perspective, but I'm unsure if my actions would have been different, as this detachment released "daddy's girl" and morphed her into woman, mother, and wife.

Eventually, I forgave him, and he forgave me. He loved me, I loved him…always, and no quarrel or misunderstanding would disrupt that. We moved beyond our separate pain and loved each other through the unimaginable hurt that awaited all of us.

Panic and pain set in and I didn't know how to tell the others. Were we really ready to face the decision we made to not resuscitate her if need be? Were we really ready to say goodbye to the baby girl for which we had so desperately prayed? Damian and I had two healthy boys and had always prayed for a baby girl to complete the Berrien Brood. I longed for a daughter to play "dress up" with, arrange tea parties with Cabbage Patch and Barbie dolls, and more importantly, wanted to see myself in someone just like me. I couldn't wait for the "Auntie's in town" menstrual discussions that my mom had with me, running awkwardly up to a middle school with a manila envelope full of sanitary napkins and tampons, leading my daughter to one of the most important decisions of her adolescent life. But, perhaps what no one, including Damian, knew was that I wanted to protect her innocence and trust; to shield her from the hands of god-bother molesters that slither up little girl's yellow dresses and poke and prod in sacred places where trust and vulnerability reside—I desperately needed to protect her from this, from one little girl to another.

Oh, but Death, its presence was felt when everyone entered her bed space. Her godmother, my best friend, hovered over her NICU crib as if warding off death's grip until we accomplished what we all purposed to do that day, but to no avail. Death was there and it was determined to accomplish that to which it was purposed. We closed the curtain and joined in song, prayer, and worship. Sanai Joi Bahndeh was dedicated to the Lord, June 11, 2011…hours before she left to be with the King.

**

It's crazy how things turn out-- one minute we're snapping pictures, holding baby girl…really enjoying ourselves, and the next minute she's struggling to catch her breath. She wasn't the same baby from that Friday night. She was so happy—playing with her brothers, looking in my eyes like she had so much to tell me, letting her mom change her clothes like a model at a real photoshoot…and not once did she have one of her "episodes". I was so proud of her that day! She conquered her condition and had a good time with all of us.

But all of that changed when I saw her that Saturday morning. Everything was different, nothing was the same. My wife was erratic (yelling at the doctors, yelling at her dad), and Sanai seemed out of it—her breathing was slow and oxygen levels turned all the way up. The peace we experienced the night before was gone.

She looked so weak, tired. Through the whole ceremony she laid there struggling to breathe. I felt bad. I wanted to fix it, help her…but there was nothing I could do. She had already said, "yes" to death and God was taking her home. We finished the Christening service and spent a little more time holding her. I couldn't bare it much longer. I had to get out, grab my boys and wait in the car…get as far away from there as possible. *I would come back*, I thought, *and hold her until she was ready to go*. But, in that moment, it was too much to take, too much to bare.

My wife found me waiting for her in the car, her mom and aunt took the boys. I don't think she noticed the stains on my face from the tears. I had tried my best to wipe them from my face. I could tell she didn't want to leave, but knew she needed to. I told her we would come back later if she wanted, knowing I had already planned on coming back anyway. She didn't want to go to her parent's house and pick up the boys; for some reason she wanted to go to her aunt's house and just "chill"…like she was waiting for something. So, we went to her aunt's house and sat there replaying the day and praying.

***

 I was blessed to share an intimate moment with her that afternoon. I held her tightly and sang as "Lord Prepare Me to be a Sanctuary" by the West Angeles COGIC Mass Choir played on her bedside radio. I was told previously by one of

her nurses that babies like to exit while being held by their mother...but I wasn't strong enough. As she rested comfortably in my arms, I whispered to her, "I know you're ready to go, but mommy isn't strong enough for you to go while I'm here, so I need you to wait." Here, a woman who is a leader at her school, in her family, in her church, and in her profession was too weak to hold her daughter as she transitioned to Glory. I was weak...that was the first time I truly realized my mortality and became angry with myself. *What kind of mother can't hold her baby during this difficult time? What kind of mother leaves the NICU and the hospital altogether knowing her baby is dying? What kind of mother thinks of herself during her daughter's death?*

As if she knew the words I spoke, her eyes widened and her heart rate increased...and she decided to wait. I left the hospital that moment knowing that would be my last interaction with her on this side of Heaven.

We got the call while at my aunt's house. The on-call doctor told us that she was on her way out, evidenced by her extremely low heart rate and breathing, and that we should begin making our way to the hospital. We purposefully delayed in going to the hospital because we realized we would rather praise than witness our daughter's last breath. We participated in one of the most powerful impromptu worship services we had ever experienced. We cried out to the Lord and sang songs, asking the Lord to send his angels to escort our baby home to her place of rest. We prayed for her peace and thanked God for her life. We prostrated ourselves at the Master's feet, begging for forgiveness and restoration. We prayed for comfort and peace, that of course would pass all understanding and would keep our hearts and minds stayed on Him.

After about 20-30 minutes, we made our way to the hospital. Just as we approached the bridge, the phone rang. I immediately passed it to Damian, who was driving to receive the long awaited and dreaded news. There was no need for words; the "Oh!" that bellowed out from the depths of his stomach said it all…she was gone. We looked up into the multi-colored sky and saw a cloud formation resembling a mountain of some sort; and it is from those hills we sought our help.

***

I didn't want to wait; I had every intention of going back, whether she wanted to go or not. I wanted to spend more time with my baby girl. But, when the doctor's called and said if we wanted to see our daughter before she died we should come then, my wife refused to go anywhere. She dropped to her knees and started crying and praying. I wanted to go. But, I knew I couldn't leave her there, in that broken state. All this time I wondered where she found the strength to keep going and doing all the things she was doing, and it was in that moment I realized where the strength came from. She said,

"we're going to pray her into Heaven and thank God for giving her to us"…and I got down on the ground with her and joined her in prayer.

The doctor called us again as we were approaching the hospital. My wife must have known what the call was about, but she passed the phone to me while I was driving. I knew what he was about to say too. Sanai was gone.

I sped even faster, trying to get there…like I could still catch her before she left for Heaven. I raced in and immediately asked to see her, hold her…I told her I would be back! The nurse told us to wait in a room called, "Lily's Room" and she would bring her in there. My father-in-law made sure he came in there with me—my wife refused. As soon as they brought her in, my father-in-law grabbed her—before I even had a chance. I sat there and watched him cry over her, my daughter, my baby. It made me mad. I wanted to hold her, by myself, without anybody's hands grabbing her. *Can't I have anything to myself? Can't I make a decision on my own? This is my child, my daughter!* But, I let him grieve too. Then, I got her. Her eyes closed, sleeping peacefully, no tubes blocking my view of her face. She felt heavier than I remember, her body was still. There was no struggle to breathe, just stillness. Even though she looked like my baby, she didn't feel like her anymore. I held her close to me and kissed her face. It was still warm.

***

We arrived at the hospital and were met by my parents and our sons. Damian went in with my dad to hold the remains of our baby girl…God didn't grant me that measure of strength. They held her in "Lily's Room" and cried over her lifeless shell. I waited with the boys in another room, crying and calling out to the Lord, left with a medley of emotions.

Calls needed to be made; swift decisions as to the lodging of her body…all while we sat in the NICU. Death had long gone, but left its bitterness behind for the family and NICU staff to taste. Everyone was sad. She had touched the lives of more than her father and I, she touched everyone she encountered in the hospital and those who heard of her story. All of us felt the void in our hearts of Sanai's departure. One statement from the NICU nurse replayed over and over in my mind, "Most young couples break up after something tragic like this. Make sure you all stay together"--a thought that was dismissed from my mind.

5 GRACE TO *LOVE AGAIN*

"Love is patient and kind. Love is not jealous or boastful or proud or rude. It does not demand its own way. It is not irritable, and it keeps no record of being wronged. It does not rejoice about injustice but rejoices whenever the truth wins out. Love never gives up, never loses faith, is always hopeful, and endures through every circumstance." 1 Corinthians 13:4-7

We became inseparable as a couple. Not only did I need him for support, but he needed me—a drastic change from where we were before.

We had always heard those wiser and married longer repeat the Biblical cliché, "don't let the sun go down on your wrath"—meaning, don't go to bed angry, especially when angry with the person to whom you are espoused. Our thoughts on the matter, "Pish, whatever!" Early in our union, we would have menial arguments over nonsense matters that would not only ruin the night for us, but damage days (and in many instances, weeks) of wedded bliss. Now when matters of the heart, such as infidelity were involved, we felt justified in evoking the "silent treatment" method to one another, which we discovered still had no merit and warranted a drastically different approach.

We were nearing our first year of marriage when my gut and heart collided with fate and a phone, all answering my inward concerns of whether or not my partner was 'stepping out' on our commitment to God. (WE later realized, it was just that: he stepped out on God. I was just caught in the crosshairs of his spiritual infidelity).

We both were home when his cell phone rang in the bedroom and the Holy Spirit sent me to answer it. It was the sound of a woman's voice that caused my heart to hit the pit of my stomach, nearly drowning it in gastric juices. She informed me that her call was one expressing frustration because after spending the night with her, her suiter—my husband—would not return her calls. Perhaps the Holy Spirit's booming resonation of dissatisfaction arrested his focus and drowned out her many calls. I watched his mirrored reflection standing beyond the bathroom doorframe, gazing in disgust at the man of my dreams. Perhaps, that too, was a conflict, because our marriage was of the 'real', not fantasy world and was inadequately viewed with dreamy eyes.

We both knew a heated discussion was lurking, awaiting the call disconnect and the igniting question, "Did you have sex with her?". We both knew any answer to that question would be deemed unacceptable, yet we both waited for its posing. So, I asked and it was met with a prompt, "No!". The story told was that he befriended a guy at the basketball court and was asked to go to a club that night. While at the club, they met some girls and were invited to "chill" afterwards. He insisted that he just watched television with her…and that was it. As expected, I refused to believe the innocence of the matter and that he return, with all his belongings to her house, so that he could continue watching TV.

We separated for weeks (even when we physically reunited, we remained spiritually and emotionally apart). The foundational elements of our marriage had shifted and we hovered on cement stilts, awaiting a foundation change. We now admit that our marriage was never based on biblical principles. We had sex before marriage, we didn't pray or study the Word together; we never requested Divine intervention with relationship concerns; and when faced at the crossroads of marriage and divorce, we scrambled looking for answers among unmarried, unhappy friends.

I believe it was at this point that we were raised and Christ repositioned Himself as the foundation of our relationship. We decided to work things out and focus more on our spiritual growth. WE joined a local church, attended membership classes and became active in the ministry. Still looming was the cloud of dishonesty and her partner insecurity. I no longer trusted his word and filled my day with analyzing cellphone billing statements, checking voicemails/ text messages and generating interrogative questions; while he spent the day defending each action, apologizing for minute offenses, and deleting evidence of unfaithfulness—because he had not fully learned from the err of his ways. Both of us were very busy. But, Sanai's illness freed us, released us from the pang of marriage offenses and focused our attention on something greater than ourselves.

So, we learned to love even when love lacked reciprocation-- we loved our children; we loved each other; and we learned to love God even more.

6 GRACE TO *STOP*

"For everything there is a season, a time for every activity under heaven. A time to be born and a time to die. A time to plant and a time to harvest. A time to kill and a time to heal. A time to tear down and a time to build up. A time to cry and a time to laugh. A time to grieve and a time to dance."
Ecclesiastes 3:1-4 ESV

No one tells you how to stop your milk after your baby dies.

I guess it's an aspect of the reality of death that pales in comparison to the actual event. For me, however, it was a significant concern. God had blessed me with an abundant supply of breastmilk during the four months of Sanai's life—so much that my mother and I filled three freezers full of the "Mother's Milk". Remember, this was the liquid gold that was supposed to heal my daughter's infirmities and make her all better…but now I was left with the dilemma of disposing of bags and bags of gold.

I sat downstairs in black, on the small step stool in the midst of unsympathetic "comfort committee" members of neighboring church groups, feeling my breast swell like water balloons. It's amazing that death doesn't tell Mother Nature to turn off the faucet because of the lack of need—isn't that the basics of supply and demand?

My mind had neglected to inform my body that its life-giving nutrients had failed and were no longer needed. Pain surged with every "comforting" hug. Even thoughts of her face, her smile, and her touch caused a surge of milk to fill my chest, adding to the physical and emotional pain. The loud crowd filling my living room had no clue, and in fact did not care about my real pain; they assumed death had visited me by itself. But it didn't. It brought with it its friends, Pain, Grief, and Anxiety. A funeral had to be planned; a casket picked; an obituary to be written; and burial clothes to be bought, all while entertaining the "Insensitives".

They wanted food, they wanted drink, they wanted the remote control to the TV, they wanted to sing songs of "grief and comfort" that I either didn't know the lyrics to or didn't want to sing. But, I did it anyway because that made them happy. They were "there for me" and I needed to show my gratitude. I wanted to offer them my milk since they were so needy, after all, I had that in abundance...patience, not so much.

It was my childhood best friend that stepped in and said, "Enough!" Baffled by the gall of the visitors, she provided choice words to redirect everyone's focus to the two parents in black with their heads hanging low...the two people who had just suffered an extreme loss. She admonished them (in a way only she could) to stop thinking about what they needed and focus on what they could help us with.

With that said, she pulled me upstairs and told me, "take off your shirt!"

This seemed like an extremely inappropriate request (for so many reasons of which I will not elaborate), and I'm guessing she realized its absurdity as evidenced in my facial expressions. She then pulled a head of cabbage and an ace bandage from her bag and held it in the air for clearance purposes. I still didn't understand, but I trusted her, so I exposed myself. She had always had my back. From the times in fourth grade when the kids picked on me because of my Jerry curl, to the times in middle school when I couldn't find genuine friends, she was there. We didn't talk every day, (we didn't need to), but we both knew we would be there for one another when the time came; and she was here for me now.

She gently placed the cold cabbage on my gorging breast and wrapped the ace bandage around my chest, packing me tightly. I didn't know if it would work, but we had to beat this fail with a try.

I was empowered to press forward. Armed with focus, I rejoined the group and sat with my husband to plan our baby girl's celebration service.

***

I knew she was having difficulty facing our daughter's death. She kept busy--from the time we left the hospital that night to the days we entertained visitors before the funeral. I was having a difficult time dealing with her death also. I mean, we didn't have time to wrap our heads around what had just happened when we were expected to pick a funeral home, decide on a date to bury her, find the money to bury her, and still try to make things normal for our boys. It was a lot.

My wife had a life insurance policy for all of us, including the kids. Not once did we think we would have to use it, but we found ourselves in the position to use our rider policy and the company told us Sanai was ineligible because she never came home from the hospital. They made it our fault that our daughter was confined to her NICU bed for the almost four months of her life and refused to pay out anything. This added to my frustration. *How was I supposed to pay for my daughter's funeral? What kind of father can't pay to bury his own daughter? Why did I let this catch me off guard?* I expected her to live, never die—and her death left me unprepared, uncertain, and unable to provide the support my family needed.

Thankfully, the hospital chaplain connected us to an organization that paid all of the expenses for Sanai's burial. I didn't have to worry about baby girl's burial; the Lord had made a way. I was able to finally grieve…something I didn't know I needed to do.

7 GRACE TO *SPEAK*

"For since, in the wisdom of God, the world through wisdom did not know God, it pleased God through the foolishness of the message preached to save those who believe." 1 Corinthians 1:21

I preached my daughter's eulogy.

It was a no brainer. We sat at the funeral home finalizing the plans for Sanai's Celebration service. We selected the cutest, most durable white casket with pink lining—as we definitely didn't want insects and worms accompanying our daughter in her final resting place. We selected the best, yet affordable embalming package, limousine, flowers, and burial plot we could find. *Who knew finding infant burial plots would pose a real challenge?* We planned the order of service together, right there with the mortician, who took special interest in Sanai's service as she, too, had an infant daughter who transitioned to Heaven when she was my age. We would have praise dancers, soloists, poems, and a farewell reflection that only a mother could deliver. We first had to survive the wake.

That was the first time Sanai's death became real for me. As that Friday approached closer and closer, I dreaded waking up. I knew that I would have to face seeing Sanai again, but as a shell of a once vibrant beautiful baby girl. I had taken careful consideration in how I wanted her to look, not really knowing how the burial body of a baby should look, but knowing I wanted my baby girl to look "normal".

My mother bought a beautiful white angelic dress and matching frilled socks for our baby girl. The sales woman asked what the special occasion was and was indescribably shocked when told it was for my daughter's funeral. Shock morphed into confusion, wondering why we would spend so much money and so much time finding the perfect outfit if it were just merely going into the ground. This would be our final goodbye—we had the money and we had the time. It was a somber, yet beautiful event— one that could only be shared with a mother for her daughter. I always thought my mom would accompany me with Sanai when she would shop for the white dress that Damian would have to give her away in, but the reverse was happening: I, as Samuel's Hannah, was giving my daughter away, back to God, in her pretty white dress. The role reversal was surreal. We dropped off her clothing, tiara and pamper at the funeral home (who knew a deceased baby would need a pamper for burial), leaving it only in the hands of the trusted mortician who had once experienced the same grief I was experiencing. Her loving smile and reassuring words, "I'm going to take care of your baby; she will look like a precious angel," comforted me.

Friday came and the idea of waking paralyzed me. I couldn't think about preparing for the Eulogy on tomorrow because I desperately needed to know that I would survive the day.

We prayed together—prayed that God would get us through breakfast; get us through lunch; get us through snacks in between, and most importantly through the wake. The day became a blur with people in and out; asking questions we cared not to answer, wanting to know things we cared not thinking about, and trying to cater to our needs, needs we couldn't articulate. We 'needed' our daughter back and none of them could give that to us.

Our boys never left our side. Grandparents, God parents, parents of friends all volunteered to "take them off our hands" so we could 'properly' grieve, not realizing that taking an alive child because of a dead child can be just as traumatic and insensitive…leaving the grieving parent with No child! We held tightly to our boys during this time. They helped in all the arrangements—even picking her frilly socks and crown. They wanted their baby sister to be pretty when she went to Heaven and so did we.

We sat in the car outside the funeral home holding hands. Our family from out of town had arrived safely and were waiting patiently for our exit to greet and comfort us. We peered through the rear-view mirror at the entrance of the chapel—what seemed like miles to walk. We were allotted an hour before the wake began to examine the arrangements to ensure our satisfaction with their services. We made it inside, but my feet were cemented to the carpet at the doorway. I could see her body from where I stood: still, under a sheer canopy, with angelic lighting. They urged me to come forward, to see how beautifully she slept. As we approached, we could smell the comforting fragrance of baby lotion, Johnson & Johnson specifically—oh how we had yearned to smell that scent one last time. She was beautiful…normal, without tubes, IV's, and bandages--a doll baby lying solemnly on a pillow of pink bedding. I had only one observation, only an error a mother would notice— her nose was made to look "normal", flat without a point and my beautiful angel had a point at the tip of her nose…and I wanted it

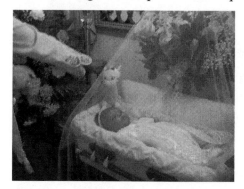

pointed again. There was nothing they could do at this point to correct their mistake, but the mortician relayed her sincere apologies for the mishap and offered words to console.

The time had come and the doors were open for the barrage of mourners that waited patiently outside to enter. Many we did not know—I later found out that the Superintendent of the school district invited all employees to attend in solidarity of the loss of their 'Teacher of the Year's' child, such a kind gesture and much appreciated. So many mourners for a small little girl that had never left her NICU bed. She touched so many lives in such a short amount of time.

***

I had to walk out of the Wake. There were too many people making it about them and not enough people focusing on my baby girl. I sat there watching all the people, many of whom I didn't know, had never seen before, didn't come and visit her while she was alive, but came when she died, that it turned me off the whole ordeal. This isn't how I wanted to celebrate her. I didn't want everyone looking at her in that small box—trying to figure out why she died, what was wrong with her, who she looked like...none of that mattered now! I didn't want to hear people get up and testify or preach...what did they know about my daughter? What could they possibly say to comfort me? How could they know how I felt in all of this when I didn't even know how I felt about it all?

I didn't know how much I needed a friend at that time, until I found myself getting angry listening to people speak over my daughter's dead body and the next thing I knew I was outside pacing back and forth. I didn't even realize my wife's former classmate/ administrator who was there when the funeral home carried my daughter's lifeless body from the hospital, had followed me outside the chapel and was there to listen to me blow off steam. The talk helped. I didn't have many male friends to vent to during this entire process, and it helped to have one now that was there to just listen. Not offer advice, just listen. I needed the validation that my anger was appropriate considering what I was facing and how my feelings were being ignored. I had remained quiet far too long.

The day we dreaded had finally arrived, the day we would bury our daughter. I didn't know if it would be understandable if I cried—you know having to be strong for everyone, including my wife and children. I felt like she would understand that I had held it in until now and give me a break to just cry, yell, curse, whatever I felt like doing. I cried. Like a man, I cried. Like a man who lost his only daughter, I cried. Like a man who would never see his daughter again, I cried. Like a man, I cried.

***

Allow me to share the words the Lord gave me to eulogize our daughter:

> "Questions, questions, questions…that's what we have in a time such as this one. One question I've wrestled with this week is 'Lord, how does a mother heal from the hole in her heart? How does a mother fill the void left behind after her child, in this case, her baby has been taken away? How can a mother heal?'
>
> I can only imagine the pain felt by Mary as she watched her son give up the ghost on a sinner's cross atop a hill. The pain she must have felt watching her son take his last breath and drop his head. The pain as she witnessed the men take his body down from a cross and carry it away to be locked and sealed in a foreign tomb…the pain once she realized her child was gone. How can a mother heal?

There's still an adverse question for this same scenario: How can a father heal?

How can a father heal from the pain of seeing his child, his only begotten son, dying a death coined for sinners, and enduring the agony of taking on the weight and sins of the world...A parent's pain so great, the Father's demeanor temporarily changed and darkened the earth and made foundations quake? How can a father heal?

The answer is simple...by realizing the purpose in pain.

It is human nature to question situations, trials, challenges, obstacles, road blocks and of course finalities such as death in our lives. It is human to correlate a cause and effect relationship to the events that occur in our lives.

We seek to find a rational reason for the pangs and disappointments in our lives...and sometimes the reason is not "rational" at all and is indeed too simple for our limited understanding.

Such was the case of the blind man spoken of in John 9. The disciples were perplexed and brought up a very interesting question to Jesus..."and his disciples asked him [Jesus], saying, 'Master, who did sin, this man, or his parents, that he was born blind?' (John 9:2).

Now, here's a man who from birth could not see. I imagine his parents had to cope with the disappointment of first realizing your child could not see your face, only hear your voice; the disappointment of having to teach your child to communicate without sight; the sadness knowing other little boys and girls would run around freely living 'normal' lives...the pain had to have been

56

present.

Now, this boy is a man and has somehow made it through life without seeing the visual manifestations of God. So, the disciples ask, is it because the man did something wrong or because his parents did? Because of course, those were the only two 'rational' options, right?

Jesus responds, "neither hath this man sinned, nor his parents…" (John 9:3). We want to know whose fault was it? Jesus answered them by saying, this thing happened so 'the works of God should be made manifest in him."

Can you imagine receiving an answer like this? This thing happened…this child was born with this defect, all so the works of God should be made manifest in him. Jesus continued, 'I must work the works of Him that sent me." (John 9:4)

So, in other words, this child was born this way not because of a specific sin committed by him or his parents, but that God would end up getting the glory of the situation. I can hear the wheels turning in the minds of the disciples asking, 'How would God get the glory out of this man's birth defect?'

God would get the glory in four ways: 1) He would create an unshakeable faith and testimony, 2) God would confound the wise, 3) God would make believers out of non-believers, and 4) God would create an atmosphere of worship (John 9:5-38)

It was all for God's glory! His ailment was for God's glory; His struggle was for God's glory; his healing was for God's glory…it was all for God's glory. There was purpose in his pain.

So, I'm comforted today because I now realize there

was a purpose in Sanai's pain. It was all for God's glory. There was nothing she did wrong, or for that matter, nothing I or my husband did wrong…it was all for God's glory.

Like the psalmist, I can hear Sanai saying, 'I will praise you; for I am fearfully and wonderfully made: marvelous are they works; and that my soul knows well. My substance was not hid from you, when I was made in secret, and curiously wrought in the lowest parts of the earth. Your eyes did see my substance, yet being unperfect; and in your book all my members were written, which in continuance were fashioned, when as yet there was none of them.' (Psalm 139:14-16).

There's a purpose in our pain; there was a purpose in her pain. He did it for our good, but for His Glory."

That was the message the Lord comforted me and all

those who mourned Sanai's passing—a message that

revealed the alignment of our pain with God's purpose,

intricately woven together by His grace. It was God's grace

that was the thread that wove the events of those four months

and our lives together, carefully crafting a testimony that

would give Him alone the glory. Grace knitted us all

together; kept us from losing focus (and our minds); it was

Grace that moved us beyond various moments of uncertainty

and anger to pastures of peace and resolve. It would be this same amazingly divine Grace that would put us in the

direction of the next phase of our witness for the Lord.

"But to each one of us Grace has been given as Christ

apportioned it." Ephesians 4:7

Lord, we thank you for Your Grace.

Damian and Youmone Berrien at their wedding reception and then 10-year Vow Renewal

ABOUT THE AUTHOR

Pastor Youmone and Minister Damian Berrien are the founders of Commissioned By Christ Outreach Church and both are ordained ministers of the Gospel of Jesus Christ. In their 12 years of marriage, the Berrien's have birthed 4 boys and Sanai, the daughter—whose life was the focus of this anointed testimony. It is their prayer that this book comforts the bereaved, encourages the discouraged and guides men and women to the light of God's grace.